Autumn, Again;
Spring, Anew

OTHER BOOKS BY SERPENT CLUB PRESS:

Autumn, Again; Spring, Anew
Michael Skelton & Stephen Morel

A Quarter Century
Eda Gasda

Circumambulate
Daniel Bossert

Moon on Water
Matthew Gasda

On Bicycling: An Introduction
Samuel Atticus Steffen

Sonata for Piano and Violin
Matthew Gasda

The Substitute
Michael Skelton

What Was Left Of The Stars
Claire Åkebrand

– And Our Journal –
New Writing: Volume I
New Writing: Volume 2
New Writing: Volume 3

Autumn, Again; Spring, Anew

Stephen Morel and Michael Skelton

SERPENT CLUB PRESS

AUTUMN AGAIN; SPRING ANEW
Copyright © Serpent Club Press, 2017
All rights reserved

Serpent Club Press books may be purchased for educational, business, or sales
promotional use. For more information please contact Serpent Club Press at:
editor@serpentclub.org

Second Edition

Printed in the United States of America
Set in Williams Caslon
Designed by Emily Gasda

ISBN
0990664309

LCCN
2014947219

Contents

1   Autumn, Again: Part I (2014)

     Stephen Morel

27   Autumn, Again: Part II (2017)

     Stephen Morel

41   Spring, Anew (2014)

     Michael Skelton

73   Estival (2017)

     Michael Skelton

Autumn, Again: Part I

Stephen Morel

1

the blurred violence of the
countryside
untranslated from what it was:

an aphoristic
photograph

bleak flowers
bleak water

(the erasure of a fallen
tree)

2

lightning buried
in the hills:

poetry must pass through the flesh like that:

(like light through a vacuum)

3

the Mind darkening
windless &
the light

of the Indian summer
unseen at the center of a

red sky

so cold
so clearcut

4

our hymns are no longer vocable
they are pure Voice &

how almost imperceptibly the oak & the elm leaves
hang like pearls from the

collarbone of heaven &

how when you began to speak to me like that I
begged for you to never stop

& you didn't

5

a single red grain persists in the void

of Time
which is

distributed evenly across the
indifferent soul

making a pattern like a bell-curve
or

like a fugue ringing in the ears

or

[2]

like a noise in the sea

crying out in anger

6

from the foam of nonexistence:

the eternity you came from is the eternity you

are going to

& many billions of stars (like people) shamelessly
starve for oxygen (you think)

7

our faces look like wallpaper flowers frozen in a
state of bloom

because you've cured

yourself with a glass of garlic & dandelion juice

& now your skin looks red and healthy exposed

to the sound of light

8

& we shouldn't fear what we don't understand
(being born into life) &

we converge
in a single Abstraction

like two awful blooms falling

from NOWHERE into
a still pool of water

9

our light will pass
through the
leaves
like
a hand
through water

10

so describe the dance-like movement of
your inner-light

as it slides from one end of the room to the other
in
the course of these afternoons
together

(because absence
is a form of radiance
you know)

11

rising through
the depths of the grass we don't encounter any
resistance on our way to becoming Total

& what we have
(what we can count on)
are small things like
moons & fishes

[4]

& Chinese-lanterns

& the sense that these things are
too precious to retain a
place inside a poem

& we could try to bring the Overall to a single
point

(but something lost there
is irretrievable)

12

a star
dying in your palms
like a bird
with a broken wing
sheds no light

13

& the Overall shuttling across the sky looks like a
giant traipsing

across a meadow &

if you want access to the ideas inside these hail-
stones you have to open them with both hands

14

because everywhere we are surrounded by linkages
&

dissolutions & images

[5]

& because a poem welcomes us
into the Open

(line: integration:
a structure of incommunicable enchantment)

15

mothers talking to children & children talking in
the voices of birds & birds talking in the voices
of angels & the transformation is never pleasing
when it occurs without our awareness of it & the
scaffolding of music is the first to collapse inside
the ear (& that's why our ears are always ringing:
because annihilation is always forgotten when we
speak from the inside)

& subject
& object
could emerge
from the
radius of the same circle
(if they wanted to)

16

a projection of some
other Voice verging on
the sacred

& the destruction of the trees signals
the end of

the life-&-death
cycle

(because
there are many renewals
contained within
a single renewal)

17

a bare house
stripped of its
mental furnishings:

a blue house
built inside an autumn star

18

pieces of sound are
falling

while

you
stand there

with your mouth open

19

our mourning is as quick as lightning to strike us &

the Mind is a healing process as much as it's a

mental process & the concussion of the

Unknown gathering inside the Known is terrifying

like a blue artillery shell

brightening over a trench

& the burden of energy is its spiritual irreducibil-
ity

(the tendency to manifest itself as a visual abstrac-
tion)

& we must exhaust the outpouring of
this Source
at its source

so we don't
betray the realization
that we are the only ones who can

20

& we (children of the stars)
are always mirroring
the Kosmos
& a paper moon
can be folded
back into a swan
if you can trace
the geometry of pain

21

cultivate a responsive-
ness towards love:
because
what we're feeling is
the zero-gravity of tumbling off the horizon of
time:

[8]

22

factors of thinking emerge to assert themselves as
True in the

vacuum of
self-realization & a fifth

can become a third as quickly as a symphony

can become a string quartet

23

this earth is as unstable as our being together
& to swallow a cloud would

be a miracle
& so would waking up to an eternity of happiness
or something like it

24

shedding ourselves of the summer & its intentions
& a

radiance is a radiance is a radiance
(& we would garner no attention
from the sky if we disappeared forever)

25

so believe me when I say our features are wholly
human for a reason
& are meant to be

symbols of

winter
& its absolution

& the cognitive
firmament is as transparent as
time is
& our miraculous self-love is not the result of any
substantial
meditation but just is & is not

more hysterical than our being here

& the more mystical the Mind gets the

more unclear
it is
as to what
It is

26

every unveiling

of autumn light is the unveiling of something in-
conceivable about the vacancy of the afterlife

& this is

not chaos but this is not order either & halfway
between limitation & limitlessness is where

you become shocked at your own serenity

&
the trees glow blue today
dying

[10]

the way they always do
this late into October

27

& the question of love is always

asked the same way everywhere

& the murmur of love is always explained as the
same
irrational
beginning of a mystery
beginning with an "I"

28

we have to insist on being ourselves

&

watching the

lightning strike down around the yard
I realize that the hush of the all-beautiful is the
hush of being alive

& look!

29

the last green trees
are holding onto their

integration with pride
& speak

o' Unspoken-For

& lean

through the invisible presence of the sun & feel

its joy

& know that the

autumn is for You
& that it breathes like
You do
(just the same)

30

we are protected by a shield of lyricism

& a trace of heaven
flashes before your unclosed
eyes

31

the leaves fall
like patterns of water around you (constellations
flowing overhead)

& you will never be
meaningless as long as you stay
where you are

(which is alone within yourself)

the foxgloves are boxing
us
in
so why don't we clip them

finally

& put them in a jar?

a way of finalizing sorrow &
making motion out of stasis &
we can locate everything wrong with
us in our failure to attain pleasure
so listen again to the wind & assure me that forget-
ting is the best method of rotation

now from major to minor key:

(shaking identity off like rain from a raincoat)

& yes! open the Soul &

edify me
dear
sustain me with your
hunger & bare necessity

& explain to me again
what we are
evolving into?

is it grace?
is it the grass
we clipped
& stacked

next to the driveway?

because

consciousness has its own
Shakespearean
way of talking to itself

just like we have our own way
of talking to
the stars

35

our way of perceiving
is an emotional mode

& we are like two mariners
on a flat-bottomed boat exploring

a moonlit sea

& this is the final
& the first Crossing

at the same time

& the shadows we

etch in the soul are no more earnest than our sand-
castles are

[14]

& we have always said we feel guilty for living
indoors but don't mean it
because the weather will always attack the founda-
tions
of the house to punish us

(so we wait & wait & wait
for it)

36

& now autumn
gives way
(finally)
to the winter
so take this
November orchid
(unsewn)
& place it back in

the burial of the spring

& let's try again with endurance

(let's try to soothe the
Dryad weeping for
its lost seed)

37

I want you to

experience humility for once
because that's what I want to do for you (help you
be humble)

& don't circle around an old broken
god & laugh
or stand up at supper &
walk out of the house
because who are we (?) to say that
we stand inside a different
church of self-survival than
everyone else does?

(or that when the
sun rises
we are the
only ones shining?)

38

selfslaughter
is a spiritual vocation

& your sense of the
numinous

has always moved me
Darling

& I know
that it's a part of me when

I enter the room
of discredited silence

(as a ritual) & shift
the furniture around to seem as if

I've really
been living here

[16]

39

the weather is incoherent & the moon is lost & we
still have a few secrets left & what composes the
otherness of Love is not mental but physical &
this alone makes us Good & the spirit will punish
what has already been redeemed because the spirit
knows that discipline is an Art

40

tell me Poet: do you see the

blank inside?

can you see the redness glowing through the frame
of the leaves?

(because
like
Emerson said
writing in his journals:

trust
that what is there is there)

41

a displaced feeling that
pain is our life

so: change the question
so change the answer
so change

the contemporary mystical framework of technological pleasure

(the association of Truth
with dissolution
& disassociation)

42

constantly and radically disappointed by the infin-
ity that

passes through us like

a wave of sound
or
a wave of water

& our opening-up is everything isn't it? to the
world

and everything

(letting the soul fall over
the autumn morning
like a shadow
over the lawn)

43

the days passing like jesters
in a deck of cards

& why are we so content to watch them pass
(the days & the suns)

?

[18]

(& what about the

faded woman
next door
who is always crying
about lost love
(as if she were a girl of sixteen covered
in enough lace & fragrance
to fill a room)

?)

44

&
it's not innocence I'm talking about

it's that inexhaustible
trace of cognitive emotion

&
what
I see of you is what you see
of me

(how the earth moves
around us
& how touch loses
its violence near the point of
absolute discretion)

expressions coined for the purpose of talking about
autumn

again

& it's raining

again

& will you speak
to the eternal

that grows &
dies
inside of each
of us
like a rose?

because as of yet
there are three modes for
saying something other than
what one means:

but all modes
are primarily ontological when
spoken as poetry

& shameless
aren't you?
my Flower-Of-The-Valley:

47

& death is a searchlight
& we are searchlights in a cold universe

& that mournful song of yours is the one you sing
to yourself

& boy o' boy is it a thirst or what?

(this strange wanting

of nothing but pure
emotional love)

48

we are self-trained in a private
language

of deep

almost unforgivable

tautology

(& if your summer teeth fall out
who will sweep them up from the floor?)

49

pass a piece of sunlight through your fingers let it

break off like a piece of the moon
or like a sorb-apple from its

branch

& tell me again what we're here for &

tell me again & then

sing it for me
Child

because after a long illness you can
sing anything you like

& you can
return
to consciousness like a
dancer entering
the spotlight
from just offstage

50

remember our letters & the wingbeat of their
laughter?

because it's impossible to come down from this
kind of dreaming

& you are always telling me
that compassionate

people are suffering people
(& they really are)

51

screen our movement

with light

[22]

betray an intuition

heal us with a cut down
through the eyes:

cut
stare:

a new
more
translucent
way of seeing:

52

a lantern swings through a
field of darkness

like a page in Emerson's
journals

turning itself
over in the Mind

53

your beautiful unspoiled
hands

opening my
eyes

54

Paraclete
you have

a sweetness
that
for me
is like
piano music

55

& remember Mozart's death
in a pauper's grave? (the
Roman jonquils & anemones
in his hair?)

56

seeds of unfallen rain
so delicate before the dawn
& say:

'bleached water
wash me clean of this
spiritual deadness

take this layer
of human skin
away'

57

& the soul
of the trees
is open to
You

58

the almond trees bare
near December:

a cloud of blossoms
swaying halfway

down the ladder
of the air

59

& nude
your world
is in ruins:

naked-footed
naked heart

60

& bring Us into
the Open:
because our nearness
means sorrow

CODA

an eveningblue dove
brings no forgiveness:
a nerve deep in the wrist
remembers the burial cold

*

& close
the eyes of the
bitter moon
above you

because
I & all the others
will love you

my
Eveningblue

(I & all the others)

*

all winter we kept
to ourselves:

curled in the sun
like
orchids

[26]

Autumn, Again: Part II

Stephen Morel

1

dreams
like nettles taking over
the garden

2

it's a Phoenix or an
Icarus (something
so doomed you'll have to
dream it over & over again
in order to bring it
back to life)

3

& there's
this spring
coiled within
our language
like the spring
inside
the seasons

4

the small wind darts like
a soul &

o' my bright mirror

birdsong comes &
goes all
day long

5

we
bury
poets
with
stones

6

because tropes
that fire
together wire
together

7

a nuanced
form capable of
bearing the immense
weight of
the heart

8

because devotion in a
notebook is not the same as
devotion in life

9

the dead edges of perception
peeled off like skin & what I'm trying to
say is that I regret so many things but
not my poems

10

& it wasn't until I reread my
journals from last year
that I realized how
unhappy I was

11

a natural world is a metonym for
the human body but the human body
also operates within the framework
of the natural world

12

I'd drive up to see you with the seasons
(passively)

kept
a diary & so forth
as I told you

&
theology is an instrument of vision

(presence withdrawn
into the guise of absence)

13

ballet shoes
like molted feathers

you were the dancer
I stripped like a chambermaid

& everything is brutal when
unthought of

14

& you
become less fragile
open to
indeterminacy & experiment

15

constellations of metaphor
scattered across the mind's dark

16

grown fat
like a gourd

in the Indian
summer

I hear
you run:

never innocent
never free

17

mass the nettles into ruin
make tea
& wait & wait & wait
your fingers
sobbing like a mourner's

18

what uprooted is

rearranged:

you are not innocent
injured
or weak
I have to say

(October violets)

regret
facing back at you like a
dog at the door

19

the
Shakespearean music
or
pressure where the hurt was a universe

20

hands bloodied
like the
color of hibiscus flower
steeped in a clear jar

21

like the ten dimensions
of string theory
the structure
of falling asleep

22

(what holds together the lusters in a poem?)

poetic acts are interrupted
suspended like waves mid-motion out at sea

(it's the lexicography of words
we appended to nights
of untallied
embryonic stars)

23

silhouettes
close to the surface
of last year's
dreams

24

dried roses
crushed into the wound
of nothing

25

name theory belief attribute:
it is
a separate formation which links
a sign to the heart

26

crept down the embankment
found your fingers
creeping through the grass
unnoticed
amidst
the falling sparks of soapy rain

27

an interior membrane that responds
to touch:

a threshold clustering
at the threshold of sight

28

a process of discovery is
a closed circle

29

like an observation plane swooping
through the emotional weather

30

write to haunt (it's the only way
you know how)

31

did you forget the feline sun
before it buried you in sleep?

(we follow the structures of memory
like music)

32

a well-known logical conundrum
postulates that our own universe is only a
nanosecond old

33

I formed
you over
lament
drew you as
a wave
teased you
into a loop
pulled you out
of time

34

dead passion
like a shadow

Daphnis choking Chloe
twisted
in the dirt

summer's exhausted
broken-glass love

35

essentialize an
unalterable
view of the brain:

follow the spiral
which curves
inside of

the
future tense

then
structure the soul out of distance

36

the sun rotting
in the grass

37

children braid
their hair with stars:

a nameless one disowns
this offence

(a nameless

One:

disowned)

38

because the heart emits a vacuum
when you seal it with disappointment

39

devastation is for
brighter angels
signaling along the
highway for a lift

40

herbs bolting
too bitter now for
anything except
peasant's tea

41

the defense of beauty by reason
(aesthetics)
& we are also thinking scars

42

cold winter day
Father stacking
firewood outside

every November has been like this
for years
moving in no direction all at once

& nothing will take you away from here
(thin as an envelope
crawling across the floor)

43

I pulled your skirt down while you sat smoking in
a chair:

then we had cathedral dreams

(wrote silence
into the general grammar of the heart)

& the birds did not recognize the winter
so they stayed
spinning like tops in the freezing trees

44

cut the body
down from its splendor
like a corpse from
the scaffold

45

since our life is mapped by the zodiac
this all makes sense

(dagger in hand
eyes on the stars)

46

copper wire
stripped of
its lining

call it back now:
the fate we cut
into nascent infatuation

47

I had no names no forgiveness
so I'm sorry
& over coffee late last night
I couldn't force myself to speak
because it was all over

48

old thoughts
begging for
new sounds

49

metaphors
enjambed
in the door

50

I heard my grandfather's rain-bruised voice
picked peonies the color of your nightdress

I looked for the person
I was
grieved for the person
you were

a decade ago

51

a fallen world sunk like
wagon-wheels in the mud

52

faces from the last century
you notice them too:
gaping in the wind
as if singing

53

something
between
earth &
melody
we call
'emergence'

54

a circle deep
in the brain where
no one is betrayed

a
mimetic shadow

a
sheet of glass about to be

punched through

(& we failed this affirmative shame)

55

the breath of Autumn's being

56

someone marvels at the figure
of the dancer you drew

57

like an Idea in a painting
(weightless)

58

Eda playing Chopin in the basement

59

categories fly away like butterflies

60

everything is
asked of us
but this
now & then

now & then

Spring, Anew

Michael Skelton

PART ONE

1

Again, anew: again meaning once more, the return of the same; anew meaning once more, in a new and different way. One deepens meaning by repetition, the other by restoration. One advances by iteration, the other by invention. Is one truer than the other? *Again*: time is an intelligible cycle made of mysterious moments. *Anew*: time defers our understanding. *Again*: time apprehends us. *Anew*: time startles us.

2

Perhaps it is not a question of correctness. Perhaps there is a time for one and a time for the other, again and anew, each in its proper moment. Again qualifies autumn, anew spring. The fall after the summer solstice is the first intimation that the seasons are in a holistic cycle, a zero sum of gains and losses of life. Only autumn has this holism in its concept. More than any other moment of the year, the September equinox turns the truth of the whole, carrying the weight of what comes before and after. The March equinox does something altogether different. Spring appears to restore life out of nothing, anew, as if what was lost during winter could be regenerated in full, and continue being regenerated, life advancing without regard for ends. Where autumn is world-weary and wise, spring is brash and ignorant, separated by summer from the fact of the sun's decline. In the course of this fourfold cycle, spring must forget what comes before it in order to give the impression of having restored life out of nothing. Moreover, it must be blind to what comes after it, so that it can send life into summer without balking at the knowledge that, come autumn, life will fold back on its gains. It is a familiar narrative: again goes with autumn and qualifies a deep, reiterated truth; anew goes with spring and denotes an insurgence of life that is necessarily forgetful, blind.

3

The four-season cycle, turning upon the word again, negates irresolution at the price of sin. Sin happens when a moment of life exceeds the healthful capacity of life's fourfold shape—its 'deific square.' Sin is life in surplus. It thrives between the summer solstice and the autumn equinox, a time when the sun is most generous, yet also starting to decline. After the autumn equinox, beauty, sin's aftermath, begins to manifest sensibly in nature. Beauty is life between sin and absolution, mournfulness revealed in appearance. Mourning is possible insofar as absolution is guaranteed. Autumn mourns sin as it prepares for the cleansing shock of winter. Winter is the guarantor of the fourfold, the fourth corner of the deific square, insuring the significance of the other seasons. It is a revelation of summer's sinful surplus, counterweighing excess with deprivation. In the months between the December solstice and the March equinox, winter erases the sins of the late summer months, absolving life so that it can experience the innocence of restoration, the drawing of the deific square anew, in spring.

4

The four corners of the deific square are ignorance, sin, mourning, and absolution. With absolution comes an unalterable ideal of justice. Life is just when it completes at the end of the cycle. Each year, the deific square encloses the word again, and life completes in a manner that is not random and chaotic, but self-actualized, possessive of meaning. This overall Again, the Again of the fourfold cycle, is greater in scope than the lesser again that belongs to autumn. Autumn arriving again is the repetition of a particular moment in a cycle that is more than the sum of its moments. Yet what about the word anew? Would it be appropriate to speak of the entire cycle recurring Anew, *in a new and different way?* What is new and different is by nature epistemologically open, not yet gathered into the known. This is perfectly acceptable for spring, the season of unintelligible beginnings. But the truth of the cycle under Again has to be the overall intelligibility that comes out of its mysterious disclosure of a guarantee. If life is insured with a guarantee, then the word Anew has to be excluded from modifying the overall cycle. The deific square cedes to sin in order to control what might be worse than sin—this unknowable open-endedness of Anew. Sin is the cost of forgetting the possibility that life, in the beginning, could as validly have been proclaimed unfair and futile, as just and worthwhile. This is the danger of the word Anew: when it trespasses beyond its proper moment in spring, it threatens the conceptual integrity of life.

PART TWO

1

The literary form that honors the deific square is the elegy, the mournful ode. The wail of the elegist does not indicate true anguish, but a deep and abiding faith that life is just. Mourning is most painful where faith is strongest. To truly mourn, an elegy must speak with unyielding faith from a dark moment between sin and absolution. The essence of faith is pre-cognitive, committing itself before the mind gets engaged. Faith nominates life as an object worthy of mourning. Life is worthy when it is bound to an ideal of justice that holds without polemic. The first element of justice must be intuitive like faith, of a higher authority, while the second element is cognitive, of a counterweight. What is this higher authority? Etymologically, to wield authority means to be able to originate from nothing, as life does when it restores itself in spring. Authority also has the power of increase, as life increases itself in the spring and summer months. A pure state of authority would demand endless originality and increase, a perennial surplus of life. Yet this surplus would be incompletely just. A second element, a counterweight to authority, is needed to render justice fully. This counterweight brings equanimity—evenness of mind—to the dispensation of authority. Justice is authority counterweighed by even-mindedness, or faith checked retroactively by thought. Yet thought does not check faith in order to undo it, but to make it intelligible. Intelligibility is a yearning for what does not need to be explained. The elegy is the voice of the mind speaking from the frontier of intelligibility, looking back upon ineffable terrain.

John Keats' 1819 poem, 'To Autumn,' sets the elegiac precedent for thought mourning faith:

Season of mists and mellow fruitfulness,
Close bosom-friend of the maturing sun;
Conspiring with him how to load and bless
With fruit the vines that round the thatch-eves run;
To bend with apples the moss'd cottage-trees,
And fill all fruit with ripeness to the core;
To swell the gourd, and plump the hazel shells
With a sweet kernel; to set the budding more,
And still more, later flowers for the bees,
Until they think warm days will never cease,
For Summer has o'er-brimm'd their clammy cells.

Who hath not seen thee oft amid thy store?
Sometimes whoever seeks abroad may find
Thee sitting careless on a granary floor,
Thy hair soft-lifted by the winnowing wind;
Or on a half-reap'd furrow sound asleep,
Drows'd with the fume of poppies, while thy hook
Spares the next swath and all its twined flowers:
And sometimes like a gleaner thou dost keep
Steady thy laden head across a brook;
Or by a cider-press, with patient look,
Thou watches the last oozings, hours by hours.

Where are the songs of Spring? Ay, where are they?
Think not of them, thou hast thy music too,—
While barred clouds bloom the soft-dying day,
And touch the stubble plains with rosy hue;
Then in a wailful choir the small gnats mourn

Among the river sallows, borne aloft
Or sinking as the light wind lives or dies;
And full-grown lambs loud bleat from hilly bourn;
Hedge-crickets sing; and now with treble soft
The redbreast whistles from a garden-croft;
And gathering swallows twitter in the skies.

Keats' poem speaks from a purgatorial moment between sin and absolution. The poet assigns two responsibilities to autumn. The first is to be steward of summer's overabundance—'Conspiring with [the sun] how to load and bless'; the second is to mourn, through music, the turning of the fourfold process—'Then in a wailful choir the small gnats mourn…' For Keats, autumn's music is a harmony of fruitfulness and loss. Choirs of gnats, bleating lambs, singing hedge-crickets, whistling redbreasts, twittering swallows, all work in concert to celebrate autumn's 'o'er-brimm'd' abundance, and to lament the turning of the now-declining year.

Yet autumn's chorus is not the only echo in Keats' ear. In the first line of the last stanza, memory of spring momentarily distracts the poet—'Where are the songs of Spring? Ay, where are they?' This is a curious interjection in an otherwise unbroken ode. Suddenly, autumn's beauty is self-conscious, diminished by a comparison to the other equinox. The comparison feels inappropriate in a poem that purports to enumerate the perfections of the season at hand, not dwell on the traits of other seasons.

There seems to be a note of competition in Keats' comparison as well, for the poet finds it necessary to reassure his September muse that its music is equally worthy of notice as spring's. And why would autumn's music need reassurance against the songs of spring, if they did not somehow threaten it? The exclamation, 'Ay, where are they?' tinges the comparison with anguish, as if autumn's orchestral splendor could potentially fall short of spring's brasher, livelier song.

The stakes of the musical competition between autumn and spring are for stewardship over beauty. To steward beauty, according to Keats' own declaration in 'Ode on a Grecian Urn,' is to steward the sole knowable truth on earth. Thus spring threatens autumn's claim to a truth that appears as mourning and absolution, replacing it with its own idea of truth as forgetfulness and ignorance. The poet's mention of spring is a skillfully suppressed doubt that mourning is truer to life than forgetfulness, and that the elegy is the proper literary form for publishing truth.

The competition between the two equinoctial seasons is part of a darker exploration of the significance of winter, the season standing between the present autumn and the coming spring. Keats dreads these long-suffering months that have the authority to decide whether to judge life mercifully or cruelly. Winter is the one season of the four that 'To Autumn' does not address: summer is 'o'er-brimm'd'; autumn is summer's 'Close bosom-friend'; spring is autumn's musical peer; yet nothing of winter. What is winter's task? Does winter absolve life, as the elegist anticipates, or does it bring disappointment? Is the task of poetry to fall elegiacally toward winter, as the mourning poet does, or would poetry do better to rise polemically out of winter, renouncing all faith in the completeness of the cycle, marking instead, with every turn of the four, not the word *Again*, but the word *Anew*, the cycle never quite repeating, but reimagining itself, year after year, in a new and different, as yet unknown, way?

3

Winter portends the separation of mind from body. Henry David Thoreau begins the third to last chapter of *Walden*, titled 'The Pond in Winter,' thus:

> After a still winter night I awoke with the impression
> that some question had been put to me, which I had
> been endeavoring in vain to answer in my sleep, as
> what-how-when-where?

Thoreau does not remain beheld to this question for long. After an unstated duration (the inestimable time between the ending of one sentence and the beginning of the next), the question put to him by the still winter night finds easy redress:

But there was dawning Nature, in whom all creatures live, looking in at my broad windows with serene and satisfied face, and no question on *her* lips. I awoke to an answered question, to Nature and daylight. The snow lying deep on the earth dotted with young pines, and the very slope of the hill on which my house is placed, seemed to say, Forward! Nature puts no question and answers none which we mortals ask. She has long ago taken her resolution.

What is the actual duration of this winter night and morning, when Thoreau is at first visited by doubt, then purged of it by Nature? Should the above excerpts be taken literally, and the reader assume that Thoreau's anecdote elapses in the course of a single night and morning, Nature handling his question immediately, as soon as he wakes to the sunrise on the windowpane? Or is Thoreau writing metaphorically here, his anecdote in actuality the accumulation of many restless winter nights and mornings without an answer to his question, the duration lasting an entire season at Walden Pond, or even many entire seasons, as time's passing in *Walden* is sometimes best interpreted?

Nature's preordained answer is to encourage the author to place his faith in what it provides, pre-cognitively, for him. The question that troubles the mind for a 'night,' Nature waives in an instant. With recourse to Nature's candid wisdom, thought needs little persuasion to revert to faith.

Thoreau is working in an unofficial tradition of wintertime philosophy. Among his predecessors is René Descartes, who sits down to write his *Meditations on First Philosophy* after he has put on his 'winter dressing gown' and gotten the evening fire going. Descartes is longer in doubt than Thoreau. It takes the former not one, but six consecutive evenings of mental labor to prove the distinction of mind from body, a distinction that is both the cause of his faith—the idea of God is alive in the mind—and the cause for his doubts—the mind can be tricked by the senses.

On the evening of the first meditation, aptly titled 'Concerning Those Things That Can Be Called into Doubt,' Descartes, like Thoreau, is troubled by his dreams:

> This [not doubting my senses] would all be well and good, were I not a man who is accustomed to sleeping at night, and to experiencing in my dreams the very same things, or now and then even less plausible ones, as [...] insane people do when they are awake. How often does my evening slumber persuade me of such ordinary things as these: that I am here, clothed in my dressing gown, seated next to the fireplace—when in fact I am lying undressed in bed!

As he studies the sensory deceptions of dreams, Descartes takes his first step toward parting mind from body, just as Thoreau's dream parted mind from Nature before he awoke to his question answered. Something about dreaming on a winter's night brings both thinkers to the abyss of intellectual crisis, without quite throwing them in. Each describes a dangerous moment in cognitive life when the mind, in dreamy solipsism, puts a question to Nature or to God, loitering in unanswered suspense, parted by a cognitive wound from the intuitions of faith.

By morning, however, both Thoreau and Descartes get their answers, and become men of faith, again. Each finds his question answered by an infinite, restorative presence, the one calling it 'Nature,' the other 'God.' Yet it is precisely the perfection of the infinite that separates the human mind from it. Perfect knowledge causes, then resolves, the mind's sufferings. When the thinker chooses to abide with an infinite, she implicitly assents to cognitive crisis— that precarious moment of delay when her question has been put, and no answer has been given.

What if—Nature and God forbid it—this delay was to continue elapsing open-endedly, and the questioner had to go on with her life, dispossessed of an answer? What if Nature and God struggled alongside the questioner, and at the end of the long winter, did not absolve the mind of its doubts, but let spring begin, Anew, before the turning of the four was complete?

Apart from justice for the mind, there is tragedy.

Tragedy occurs when the inquiring mind asks a question and receives no answer. Tragedy is foremost a cognitive experience, since the mind must first have formed an intelligent question in order for an answer to be missed. Dispossession is a deferral of absolution. Absolution defers when the mind falls out of pace with the rest of life and fails to rejoin it. Freezing is the physical expression of the mind falling out of pace. Ice provokes contemplation. When the earth freezes during winter, and the atoms of life are stalled, the mind discovers its own unceasing motion, and begins to doubt the validity of that which is not perennial. Upon this discovery, the mind parts itself from the rest of life in order to steel itself against the stillness surrounding it. This parting is enacted through a question that thought puts to faith. When an answer is not received instantaneously, by way of an extant higher authority, the question has the effect of leveling the questioner. The first sense of *to level* is to destroy, to raze to the ground. The mind deprived of truth is masochistic. It does violence against itself by questioning the primal intimations of faith. And yet the second sense of *to level* is to bring to balance. The masochistic mind may be violent, but it is also its own authorizer, subordinate to none. It is therefore guilty before none and need not repent for having doubted. Insofar as it is unrepentant, the mind is indifferent to the pull of higher authorities. This indifference nudges the mind to strive for impartiality in judgment. What seeks impartiality seeks justice also. The leveling effect of dispossession, therefore, is an inverted articulation of justice, originating in the autonomy of the mind. What is level, indifferent, and autonomous is insofar democratic. Winter's revelation of cognitive motion is a democratic revelation of justice out of dispossession. The mind dispossessed of an answer must deduce epistemological authority horizontally, of itself, rather than vertically, of an infinite and incomprehensible other. It follows that the democratic ideal is of dispossession, not of absolution. Democracy is borne from prolonged mental winters that conclude incompletely, the main questions left unanswered. Yet the democratic winter does not prove the mind's resilience so much as the mind's enfeeblement under winter's thumb. Winters without absolution damage the mind, wounding it against life.

PART THREE

1

The literary mode of tragedy is the polemic. The polemicist is on the one hand a complainant, on the other hand, an autodidact. As complainant, the polemicist laments having to inherit thought after it has parted ways with faith. Her complaint is that the life of the mind is retrograde, impossibly inclined toward a faith it never knew and, now that the two have been divided, can no longer hope to possess. The faithless are disconsolate. While the elegist mourns past sins committed, the polemicist keens for lack of opportunity. Untouched by sin, the complainant has a totally inverted sense of what a life freely lived might be. Whereas the freedom of the elegist is to mold thought in the image of faith, kneeling at winter's forgiving altar, the freedom of the polemicist, since she has been allocated nothing, is to cognitively self-determine her own ends, pledging allegiance to the coming spring. As her freedom is concerned, the polemicist is not only a complainant, but also an autodidact, and the antithesis of absolution is not only dispossession, but also education. Those from whom mercy is withheld are let to teach themselves. Coddled by no authority, the way of their education is necessarily negative, ironic. An ironic education unfolds in two phases. The first phase is exposure to the crisis of incompletion. Dispossession teaches what it is like to be guaranteed nothing; out of nothing, irony quickens in the mind. The second phase of an ironic education is *humiliation*—from the Latin *humus*, ground—which connotes a leveling to the ground.

A sound polemic is a complaint that levels its object in both a destructive and a democratic sense. Unlike the elegy, which seeks to apprehend and honor justice, the polemic is an ironic simulation of faith, justice out of nothing, seeking with every aggrieved word to invoke a new order and to forget its complaint against life.

2

The quintessential polemic in American letters is Ralph Ellison's 1952 novel, *Invisible Man*. The novel's protagonist, the Invisible Man, is a young, disillusioned black man speaking from 'hibernation,' making his metaphorical social invisibility literal by withdrawing into the sewers of Manhattan, where he can think his own thoughts without feeling compelled to placate the undemocratic society that torments him above ground. In his subterranean schoolhouse, he teaches himself ironies that bring his existence back to sufferable terms. The goal of his ironic education is at once noble and narcissistic. He will tell his story, down to the last humiliating detail, because he believes his life is important enough to make of it a problem for others to consider.

With *Invisible Man*, Ralph Ellison discovers two essential elements of the tragic conception of life. The first is that the terms of dispossession become, perversely, the terms of freedom. Above ground, the Invisible Man's life was made miserable by his compulsion, at once conscious and unconscious, to placate others' expectations of a black person's proper comportment in public life. To play this placatory role felicitously, he had to suppress the originality of his own intelligence, lest he give the impression of being a misfit or a rabble-rouser. When he goes underground, the Invisible Man rediscovers the cause of his aboveground immiseration—*'the mind, the mind'*—and from his personal cognitive misery, creates a polemic that focuses on the problems of humanism and democracy more generally, as if to imply that the individual life, *his* life, touches upon universal themes, the bare unit substituting for the whole.

The Invisible Man recycles his dispossession as privilege by offering up his life as a metonym. Yet by no means is metonymy a state of freedom without responsibility. Insofar as the unit claims to name the universal, the former becomes disproportionately responsible to the latter. In a deep sense, the dispossessed person is the most cognitively burdened, much more so than those whose intuitions prove them correct on a regular basis. Abandoned to the mind, it is the disconsolate who must teach the faithful that the tragic sense of life is the sole sufferable one, and, moreover, the sole *defensible* one, once the truth of dispossession has been proved. The Epilogue to *Invisible Man* defends a tragic conception of democracy on the presumption that without tragedy, politics, like the narrator's metonymic life, would be utterly without aspirations. If 'humanity is won by continuing to play in face of certain defeat,' then humanity should not belong to those unmindful of tragedy. Blind faith, according to the narrator, does not encourage ongoing humanization and democratization. Despondency, however, does.

The Invisible Man's last words are carefully chosen. 'Who knows,'—he asks—'but that, on the lower frequencies, I speak for you?' His polemic concludes not with an answer but with a new unanswerable question, which he puts to his reader from the vantage point of freedom. The Invisible Man's freedom is his dispossession, recycled as privilege. His privilege is that he can make a metonym of his tragic life, naming the democratic universal with the personal. Part of this privilege is putting questions to his peers that upset their faith in the basic justice of public, not to mention spiritual, life. 'There's a stench in the air,' he writes, 'which, from this distance underground, might be the smell either of death or of spring—I hope spring.'

Which shall it be, he asks from below—death or spring, Anew?

3

Is a polemic beautiful like an elegy? If so, the definition of beauty would have to be reconstructed as the appearance in the sensible world of dispossession, recycled as privilege. Beauty would have to reveal a form of freedom that self-determines out of nothing. Such counterintuitive thinking would have to be hedged retroactively against intuition. The polemic, however, is faithless and mistrusting of intuitions. Thus the polemicist has no choice but to argue against the apparent indisputability of intuitively beautiful appearances. Beauty in its polemical form has to be screened by thought before it can appear in the world. Thought does not screen beauty to control it, but to cognize it, and to pass a judgment on it. A judgment is nothing more than a claim supported by reasons. Beauty must be defended with reasons, lest it be degraded to a fetish. The word fetish recalls the Latin word *facticius*, which in English became factitious, 'artificially made.' Intuition makes beauty a fetish by failing to come to its defense. Consequently, the most intuitive is not the truest to beauty, but the most given over to artifice. Whereas what follows from judgment, while counterintuitive, labors toward the end of letting beauty be. A sound judgment proves that the beautiful must be cognitively earned before it can ever become common sense. Letting beauty be is a skill acquired through an aesthetic education of the mind.

An aesthetic education trains the mind to judge beauty counterintuitively. The hallmark of an aesthetic education is the ability to discern between an elegy and a polemic—between art that follows an eloquent intuition of beauty, and art that makes a laborious judgment of it. The distinction is less substantial than temporal. An elegy apprehends beauty in the instant; a polemic finds beauty in delay. The instant offers a straightforward edict; the delay, an education in cunning. An aesthetic education persuades the mind by cunning. The word cunning originates from an Old Norse noun, *kunnandi*, which means knowledge. In Middle English, *kunnandi* became *can*, connoting erudition. Over time, as *can* became *cunning*, the word evolved to connote deceit. Aesthetic education is analogous to the transformation of *can*, erudition, into *cunning*, deceit. The mind is ingenious to the degree it is capable of deceiving itself with its own judgments. Far from being a deliberate recollection of what is already known, aesthetic education is willful self-deception in judgment, cunning applied against intuition, to no known end.

PART FOUR

1

Spring, Anew. Over Riverside Park, the afternoon sky glares gunmetal, a distinctively mid-March color that hints it is neither winter anymore, nor spring quite yet. The sycamore and the sky are of one hue, as if the tree were the barely concealed skeleton of the earth, holding the Overall in place. Though not yet green, cautious leaf-buds are forming along the sycamore's branches, and its roots, after months in dormancy, are quivering in the ground. By all appearances, the tree is on the cusp of resurgence. And yet it would be just as valid to assert that the sycamore still bears a look of wintry ruin, scarred bone-deep by the cold. The tree's bareness divides it from its surroundings, its profile not conforming with the mid-March colorscape, but negating any relation to it at all. The sycamore's simultaneous conformism and distinctiveness are most apparent on days like today, just before the March equinox, before the air has gotten consistently warm and spring advanced beyond regress. In a few weeks' time, however, the sycamore's cautious leaf-buds will be modest green leaves, neither in obvious conformism, nor in notable contrast, with the colors around them. A trace of winter will inhere in the greening body, for while it does have a heartier look once its leaves come in, in fact its foliage spreads pretty sparsely along the branch, the robust trunk uncrowded by the bloom, so that even at the height of June health, the sycamore will have failed to thaw its winter skeleton back to life.

*

In the periodic silences that settle over East River Park, the only audible sound from the quay is that of the ice floes colliding and cracking as they drift with the slow, but quickening, current. As the larger floes melt, they break into smaller chunks that, haphazardly drifting, ram against each other, collecting into random, angular masses that float together for a few minutes or hours before dissembling downriver. These temporary floating sculptures are best viewed at twilight, when the electric reflection of Manhattan's Lower East Side beams down to the river, hitting the sculptures at oblique angles, so that blue shadows form on the broad-faced floes, and the silhouettes of the sculptures shimmer yellow with light. Often, two sculptures will drift ashore at the same time and pin each other against the quay, stalling there, warming under the light, until one of them melts free and dissolves into partial shadow. This process will continue for a few more days until every floe rejoins the current, at which point Manhattan's electric reflection will show unobstructed on the water. Yet a certain effect will have been lost in the change. Twilit evenings will no longer witness the yellow shimmer of the ice sculptures as they stall against the quay. For once the East River's current warms to speed, the reflections of Manhattan's towers will become monotonous mirages on its brackish surface, fodder for postcard kitsch, banally reiterated in every drop of water that passes through their undiscriminating light.

2

Easter arrives just as the first golden leaves are breaking on the willows that border the creek on the west side of town. The sagging boughs crimp the sunrise in pale threads, weaving a canopy of leaves and light above the creek. Up the hill, the streets are packed with solemn traffic, mostly young families and elderly people observing the Easter holiday, driving or walking to nine a.m. worship. Many in the throng look under-rested, particularly the mothers with small children, yet many, if not most, of the elderly, look positively placid and ready to spend the next hour fishing for souls in the name of the resurrected Christ. Besides the churches, the town's other locus of activity is down the hill, at the creek bordered by willows. A handful of sturdy men toting fishing tackle and beverage coolers have distributed themselves evenly along the banks, performing their Sunday sacrament with a reverence to rival that of the Christians. And were it not for the fact that it is Easter morning, and were it not for the near-uniform goatees framing the studied frowns on the men's faces, and were it not for the ethic of silence that pervades their maritime ritual, these men might, as a group, pass for an accidental fraternity of free-thinkers, united by their abstinence from rituals that complicate Man's communion with Nature. But that is not quite how they appear. While humble of presentation, these men look more like a fraternal order than a ragtag cadre. The gender exclusivity of the group, while not inherently sexist, betrays a preference for organization over spontaneity. Moreover, these men do not appear to be seeking total solitude, otherwise they would not be fishing in the public stream. They are here to see their fellows, to be in a place where two or more of the same kind are gathered in the name of the resurrected spring. They are fishing for fish, while their neighbors at the churches go fishing for men. The difference between fishers of fish and fishers of men is one of quantity, rather than quality. After many Easter mornings of worship, these men have no additional questions to put the stream. They know just as well as the Christian what it is to be saved.

*

The Moravian Christians who came to America were humble before God and before one another and so marked their graves with plain stones that laid flat upon the ground. In a Moravian cemetery, there are no monuments or private mausoleums. Every stone is identical in size and shape, just as every individual soul is of equal measure on God's just scale. Easter morning witnesses an annual demonstration of this principle, as a few of the town's remaining Moravian descendants gather at the old cemetery for the tradition of placing flowers on the graves of children. The tradition has a profoundly democratic as well as a religious feeling. Even the gravestones of stillborn infants, who never lived an hour outside their mothers' wombs, are lavished with lilacs, their souls weighed equally with the rest.

The lilacs left on the stones are the sole adornments in a burial ground that is notable for its perfect symmetry and humble plainness. The cemetery is exactly a square city block in area, divided by two walking paths that bisect each other in the shape of the cross. The four sides are bordered by a prudent black fence that has no main entrance, but which provides two cater-cornered gates that are not gates at all, merely gaps in the fence-line, three feet in width, at the northeast and southwest corners of the grounds.

Judging solely by the design of their cemeteries, the Moravians might have been a sect that imagined God had arranged life on a divine grid, a deific square within whose enclosure each individual was a countable unit of the infinite. Their uniform gravestones were their method of keeping the tally as they waited for God to unburden them of trying in vain to understand His divine calculus. Identification with God was the source of the Moravians' mathematical identicalness to one another. Their self-leveling imitated a Being that enumerated individuals as vulgar integers long before He assigned them proper names.

But until the faithful are unburdened of the task of counting to infinity, their tallying, however great, will never be enough. Inevitably, a democracy of the faithful will feel the need to flatten itself under the burden of God's innumerable mercies. Perhaps this is why, apart from the inherent historical value of the tradition, the descendents of the Moravians continue attending to infants who died in 1863, 1877, 1894, 1903. Perhaps if these children had survived and lived full lives, the tally might have filled the grid, or at least have been further along, and the heaviness of identicalness— the dead weight of a stone—might have been lifted from their minds, allowing them to imagine a life beyond piety.

After every child's stone has been decorated with lilacs, the attendants gather in the center of the cemetery for a closing prayer. The ceremony ends with a silent single-file procession that exits through the gate at the southwest corner of the cemetery, dispersing onto the campus of the adjacent Central Moravian Church, where, out of the open doors of the sanctuary, the pipe organ booms the first note of the opening choral, and the Easter worship hour commences.

3

Wallace Stevens' poem, 'Meditation Celestial & Terrestrial,' concerns the difficulty of understanding the passage from winter to summer.

It might be re-titled, in symmetry with John Keats, 'To Spring':

> The wild warblers are warbling in the jungle
> Of life and spring and of the lustrous inundations,
> Flood on flood, of our returning sun.
>
> Day after day, throughout the winter,
> We hardened ourselves to live by bluest reason
> In a world of wind and frost,
> And by will, unshaken and florid
> In mornings of angular ice,
> That passed beyond us through the narrow sky.
>
> But what are radiant reason and radiant will
> To warblings early in the hilarious trees
> Of summer, the drunken mother?

As in Keats' 'To Autumn,' Stevens' poem devolves upon a comparative question. Keats' question—'Where are the songs of Spring? Ay, where are they?'—compares the beauty of the two equinoxes from a moment between sin and absolution. Stevens' question—What is radiant reason to drunken summer?—compares the authority of the two solstices during the final forgetful weeks of spring. A rephrasing of Stevens' question to match Keats might be: have we begun anew out of absolution or dispossession?

The lightness of phrasing is what makes the question so effective. It can be taken in several directions at once. One valid take is that the poet's question is meant to be rhetorical, and by comparing the cognitive hardships of winter to the drunken hilarities of summer, he means to endorse indolence ahead of industry. Another, equally valid, interpretation is that the form of the question is meant to inspire a counterintuitive reading, one that accounts for the whole poem instead of isolating a single moment. The counterintuitive reading accepts the question at face value—but what is winter to summer?—and patiently reviews the evidence. Winter is 'will, unshaken and florid' compared to 'wild warblers.' It is 'bluest reason' compared to 'hilarious trees.' It is 'radiant will' compared to the 'drunken mother.' Juxtaposing these associations, is one indisputably better than the other? Is a 'lustrous inundation,' for some inarguable reason, very preferable to 'angular ice,' even if the former inebriates the mind, while the latter invigorates it?

In a counterintuitive reading, Stevens' question, like Keats', retains its comparative openness. And, also like Keats, Stevens' poetic levity disguises an underlying seriousness, suggesting that the author, where spring is concerned, prefers cunning to mourning.

4

Can the smell of grass be cunning? It depends where the grass grows.

In the uptown Manhattan neighborhood of Washington Heights, a steep declivity that overlooks the Hudson River is home to Trinity Cemetery, the only active cemetery left in Manhattan. Since the cemetery ran out of pre-orderable burial space years ago, the management has been selling aboveground crypts that are located in a public mausoleum at the foot of the hill. The crypts are expensive, inaccessible to the majority of the 60,000 people who die in New York City every year.

Like most solutions to Manhattan's social problems, the mathematics of burying the dead is cold as ice: no space, no new plots. Or, now that the aboveground crypt is an option at Trinity: no money, no plots. Even the dead get gentrified in New York.

But supposing class issues were not in play, and the housing crisis of the dead were simply an issue of geography, there would still be too little ground for too many people. This definition of the problem casts the extravagant private crypts and towering monuments-to-self of bygone Astors and Hamiltons in a troubling light. Wealthy nineteenth-century Manhattanites seem to have had no foresight at all when it came to constructing their final resting places. They built too big, too early. Didn't they ever stop to consider those who were to follow them in death, legions of unborn New Yorkers who will have loved the city just as much as they loved it, and who will have wished, just as they wished, to make an eternal home in it?

Of course they didn't think about that—just look at the graves. Yet the presence of swanky stones amid spatial scarcity is no longer the thing to notice about Trinity Cemetery, not now that the solution to the problem—aboveground crypts—follows the same free-market, 'pay to decay' logic of New York's nineteenth-century elite. Nowadays, what is more pressing than the literal class politics of burial, or even the fantastical art on some of the older monuments, is the smell of the grass that grows upon the graves. Near the 154th Street summit, there is a secluded knoll that by early May starts to give off a humid, vinegary scent not unlike the scent of human perspiration on cotton clothing. The grass sweats. It sweats on the graves of Trinity Cemetery just as it would sweat on the dandelions of Ohio hillsides, or on the feet of palm trees in rural Florida. The smell of the sweating grass is dewy and warm, with a bite of tart that makes it a taste as well.

'And if nothing more,' the Invisible Man reports from underground, 'invisibility has taught my nose to classify the stenches of death.' It is early May, the air is balmy, the grass is sweating on the knoll. What is there to disqualify this as one of the many 'stenches of death'?

Indeed, what keeps the nose from sneaking a whiff of death on a sunny noon in May? And what keeps the mind from judging afterward: This is the stench of spring, Anew.

Michael Skelton
Cincinnati, Ohio

ESTIVAL

Michael Skelton

0

The rivalry between the two solstices is in full view at the French Impressionism gallery in the Metropolitan Museum of Art, Manhattan, where the curators have hung side-by-side two seasonally themed Claude Monet paintings to encourage a comparative viewing. On one side is a painting called "Morning on the Seine near Giverny," which shows the Seine winding through a forest at dawn on a summer's day. Next to it is a painting of the same scale called "Ice Floes," an image of a rural section of the Seine on an overcast morning in winter. The color palettes of the two paintings are exactly the same but with different distributions and intensities of color. In the summer image, bold greens, purples, and blues prevail over more than half the canvass, filling in for trees, shade, and darkened waters. The blended colors smear the distinction between shoreline and waterline on most of the canvass, and thus the distinction between the objects on the bank and their reflections in the river. The surface of the Seine is only visible as such at a nexus in the center-right of the painting, where the light of the rising sun flows, tendril-like, from sky to earth, the river then shuttling the morning light as far as it runs, terminating at the bottom edge of the canvass. The legibility of the entire painting hinges on this narrow channel of light and light reflected, without which it would be difficult for the viewer to sort out the lines and figures that give form to the image of a river bisecting a teeming forest.

In the winter painting, by contrast, a dusky light, made of white paint inflected with softer greens, purples, and blues, covers most of the canvass, showing a snow-white Seine and a dark cluster of trees in much clearer delineation from each other than in the summer work. The artist lets the scattered ice floes floating on the river's surface do much of the distinguishing work, rendering them with rough, amorphous strokes that separate them, not so much by color as texture, from the rest of the image. An island in the middle of the river hosting a copse of birches adds to the barren clarity of the scene, the roughed-up snow breaking definitively with the wisp-like trees rising out of it. On the whole, juxtaposing "Ice Floes" with "Morning on the Seine" encourages the insight that visual perception is more acute amid the impoverished colorscapes of winter than the comparatively richer ones of summer. The estival imagination, rinsed daily in a palette of nourishing paints, in the end has much more in it of dreaming than mindfulness.

0

Spring, anew, then summer, a dream. How is it that the most undaunted of the four seasons, known for generating life in surplus, can be known, at the same time, for inducing lethargy and sleep? That summer is characterized by its solstice seems as good a starting point for thinking as any. Solstice in Latin means "stationary sun." Summer and winter have this stationary sun in common, though at competing extremes. Winter's solstice brings about a world-freezing that enables the mind to discover itself, for the first time, as a source of perpetual motion, actuating its capacity for willing against nature's forces. Summer's solstice, by contrast, brings about a world-flourishing that prevents the mind from distinguishing nature's motion from its own. In the absence of a perceptible difference between natural and cognitive motion, the mind settles into a state of assent, moving with nature, rather than against it. Via assent, the mind agrees to be in total union with its world, joining with a surplus of life that, over time, atrophies the dissenting will.

The summer solstice steers the mind toward sleep, and dreams. *Twilight* is its sedative. Around the solstice come the longest evenings of the year, and with the prolonged evenings, the blurring of all clear and distinct objects in the visual field. Twilight is an hour when light struggles against reflected light, the setting sun competing with its own reflection in the rising moon. Figures formerly sharp and still in the daylight now start to quiver at the edges, objects with their evening shadows combine, fireflies, signaling to each other through the confusion, raise up false torches in the air. The imagination takes over the mantle of conscious thought, inducing the mind into a dreamlike state not unlike intoxication.

During the hundred-odd days between the June solstice and the September equinox, time winds itself up in a circle. Every moment that passes, rather than tallying up the hours, merely marks the felt drag of an empty duration. Here there is no steady progress of kept hours, only the *synchrony* of experience without memory, confirming the cryptic wisdom of Ecclesiastes, that there is nothing new, because nothing past, under the sun. Summer's synchronic repetitions are so unmemorable, in fact, that they seem to recur every time as if for the first time. In this regard they are not even repetitions; they are more like vanishing instants from which no lasting insights, only impressions, can be gained. Under conditions so hostile to memory, the mind develops a propensity to erase phenomena as soon as it perceives them, nulling, over time, its in-built facility for learning. The mood thus created is a composite of agony and liberation: agony, because experiencing without remembering is a kind of ecstatic suffering; liberation, because the mind's seeming indeterminability within time gives it the illusion of being freed from all mortal constraints.

0

Hubris is the word for the agonistic mental freedom experienced during the summer months. Hubris arises from the mind's sense of timelessness upon assenting to nature's motion. Its desideratum is the indefinite continuation of freedom in an everlasting summer. Such a freedom would be attainable only if summer could conquer its rival solstice–in other words, only if summer could absorb winter into itself, thereby preventing the world-freezing that gives rise to the dissenting will.

Hubris hints at the conspiracy between authority and anarchy in summer's concept. June's struggle to domineer over December year-round is an attempt to abolish seasons altogether, for an indefinitely prolonged summer would just be a state of seasonlessness, that is, anarchy in time. Anarchy is summer's total authority transformed. June's domination of December compels it to assimilate winter's tendencies into itself. Eventually, the process of melting winter's ice down to water transforms summer's original character beyond recognition. As a consequence, the annual calendar ceases to disclose any meaning, while thought, moving apace with these anarchic developments, achieves a freedom so unbounded that it admits of no limitations whatsoever on its activity.

William Shakespeare's *A Midsummer Night's Dream*, while named for summer, is really a comedy of the two solstices falling out of joint. The rivalry of Oberon and Titania, respectively king and queen of the fairies, might be read as an analogue of the rivalry of winter and summer. Titania's speech to Oberon in Act II offers a poetic summary of the confusion created by their struggle for the upper hand in their magical romance:

> Therefore the winds, piping to us in vain,
> As in revenge, have suck'd up from the sea
> Contagious fogs; which, falling in the land,
> Have every pelting river made so proud,
> That they have overborne their continents:
> The ox hath therefore stretch'd his yoke in vain,
> The ploughman lost his sweat; and the green corn
> Hath rotted ere his youth attain'd a beard:
> The fold stands empty in the drowned field,
> And crows are fatted with the murrion flock;
> The nine men's morris is fill'd up with mud;
> And the quaint mazes in the wanton green,
> For lack of tread, are indistinguishable:
> The human mortals want their winter here;
> No night is now with hymn or carol blest:
> Therefore the moon, the governess of floods,
> Pale in her anger, washes all the air,
> That rheumatic diseases do abound:
> And thorough this distemperature we see
> The seasons alter: hoary-headed frosts
> Fall in the fresh lap of the crimson rose;

And on old Hiems' thin and icy crown
An odorous chaplet of sweet summer buds
Is, as in mockery, set: the spring, the summer,
The childing autumn, angry winter, change
Their wonted liveries; and the mazed world,
By their increase, now knows not which is which:

The weather responds to the fairies' feud by making a satire of chronology. Absent any seasonal mechanism for organizing time, the annual calendar falls into chaos, as do the organic processes associated with it. The earth becomes "mazed" and unnavigable, and the otherworldly moon, "governess of floods," goads the general fury. Total inundation is nature's answer to the fairies' hubris, calling up "pelting rivers," turning arable fields to rot, but also, as if in mockery of everyone's confusion, reviving things which would otherwise be dead. Water is the medium of the meteorological anarchy described in Titania's verses, the protean element present whenever the seasons wish to trade in their "wonted liveries" for other attire. Water, by her cautionary account, is equally capable of ruining or resurrecting life, depending.

0

Summer begins to lose its hold on the mind once the September equinox announces autumn's arrival. The equinox brings incontrovertible evidence that the sun, while appearing to rule unchecked, has been steadily on the wane since reaching its highest point in June. What appeared to the sedated mind, across a hundred-odd days, as summer's never-ending health, reveals itself now, in the mellowed energies of autumn, to have been a reversible achievement. With autumn's first enduring chill, the summer dreamers start to shiver awake. Those first to rise are first to see the world in decline around them, and in the interest of saving their loved ones from the same grief, take measures to prevent them from waking. Christina Rossetti's "Dream-Love," a poem that anticipates summer's failure to persevere past the autumn equinox, explains how an illusion of everlasting summer might be artificially achieved:

> Young Love lies dreaming;
>   But who shall tell the dream?
> A perfect sunlight
>   On rustling forest tips;
> Or perfect moonlight
>   Upon a rippling stream;
> Or perfect silence,
>   Or song of cherished lips.
>
> Burn odours round him
>   To fill the drowsy air;
> Weave silent dances
>   Around him to and fro;
> For oh, in waking
>   The sights are not so fair,
> And song and silence
>   Are not like these below.

Young Love lies dreaming
        Till summer days are gone,—
Dreaming and drowsing
        Away to perfect sleep:
He sees the beauty
        The sun hath not looked upon,
And tastes the fountain
        Unutterably deep.

Young Love lies drowsing
        Away to poppied death;
Cool shadows deepen
        Across the sleeping face:
So fails the summer
        With warm, delicious breath;
And what hath autumn
        To give us in its place?

In the world of Young Love's sleep, degrees of light are indistinguishable from one another, times of day negligible, painting an overall aesthetic field that is far less legible—yet also more beautiful—than that of waking experience. "In waking," writes the poet, "the sights are not so fair," as if to imply that the sensuous slumber in which Young Love passes the summer months, while obscure in most details, protects him from having to witness the year's inevitable decline. Dreaming, then, is always an illusion of summer's everlasting splendor. Summer fails, just like the rest of the seasons. Christina Rossetti's answer to this failure is darkly comic. Instead of leaving Young Love to wake to autumn

-

naturally, so that he can encounter the death of the year on his own terms, the poet plays the puckish fairy, introducing a series of aesthetic tricks into the scene in attempt to keep the boy's midsummer dream alive. The poet burns incense, weaves dances, draws up a curtain of evergreens–in sum, builds a protective theater around the boy's mind–so that, when the season ultimately fails him, he will not wake to find his illusion interrupted.

0

The evasion of imminent tragedy with aesthetic deception is the founding act of all *comedy*. Comedy is a reflexive response to the creeping feeling of disenchantment that comes with the autumn equinox. In autumn, the mind melancholically withdraws its assent to nature, relapsing into a state of *faith* that parts it irreparably from its object. The comic poet's method, therefore, must be the total aesthetic illusion, and her aim to thwart the mind's relapse into faith by preserving the feeling of total psychological union with nature. The specific quality of illusion that comedy seeks to preserve is the indescribable sensorial plenitude. Illusion scrambles the laws of waking perception, not to mention the functions of the senses themselves–the eye accordingly believing that it hears, the ear that it sees, the hand that it tastes, and so on. The dreaming brain permits this random rearranging of the senses, each sense discovering its own power through all the others, until it becomes virtually impossible to trace the source of any given perceptual datum that impresses itself on the mind. The ineffability that results from the breakdown of sense serves comedy's deceptive purposes well: as long as a confusion persists in the mind regarding the organization of world and time, the work of faithfully mourning summer's failure does not begin.

0

The Delacorte Theater in Central Park, host every year to the Public Theater's Shakespeare in the Park summer series, must be one of the few places in the modern world where the comic ethos of *A Midsummer Night's Dream* can be properly realized in a live outdoor setting. Location has a great deal to do with the Delacorte's success. The theater's embeddedness within a garden within Manhattan easily summons the enchanted geography of the original script, which moves back and forth between an ancient Athens that resembles a composite image of that city's golden democratic centuries and a magical forest that serves as a rehearsal space for the comic performances that enliven urban life. Starting the show at twilight is another essential element of the production's success. In the gathering dark of Shakespeare's Garden, modern Manhattan becomes synchronic with ancient Athens, and the players actually become self-illumining fairies and lovers flitting under the forest's kneeling boughs. The sense of intimacy between script and world contrived here suggests less of verisimilitude than of metatheater. For it is by the theatrical medium alone that the audience is able to register the meaningful identification of Manhattan and Athens. The "dreaming" that happens within the play is in this respect the comic analogue of the "real" spectatorship that happens in the live outdoor theater. Hippolyta's flash of insight in Act V of *Midsummer* dispels all doubt that the shared medium of dreaming is what binds together the disturbed visions of players and spectators, who, despite having been tricked, hoodwinked, and hypnotized in every way during their night in the forest, manage, upon returning to the city by morning, to weave a coherent story from their confusion:

> But all the story of the night told over,
> And all their minds transfigur'd so together,
> More witnesseth than fancy's images,
> And grows to something of great constancy;
> But, howsoever, strange and admirable.

0

Western discourses on cosmopolitanism have often found the universal element of human politics in a certain orientation toward the sun. The path of the sun across the sky, as well as the reach and intensity of its light in different parts of the habitable earth, have been viewed as determinants of human political and historical development since antiquity. Ancient Roman cosmopolitans, for example, identified two distinct commonwealths–one conventional, one natural–to which all human beings necessarily belonged. The *res publica*–"one's Athens or Carthage," as Seneca put it–conferred political citizenship on human beings, providing a needed particular context for the execution of duties essential to the flourishing of local communities. The *commonwealth of the sun*, by contrast, conferred human beings a place in an undying, universal nature, and thus a means of surviving the fickle life-cycles of cities. The sun far more than the city was believed to have a gathering effect on the community of being. Its compressing of the earth's myriad peoples into a single natural commonwealth fostered the sense that nature's universality belonged to everyone as if it were something particular to each. Athens would come and go, Carthage wither, yet the true public, blessed by the sun's constancy, would go on living forever. Indeed, the Roman cosmopolitans seem to have taken it for granted that absent an indestructible natural community to survive the political community, there would have been no foundation for the ethical relations among, or for that matter within, particular peoples, nor for the ethical relationships between the self and the cosmos overall.

The actual cognitive performance of cosmopolitanism involved a mental compressing of cosmological space called *oikeoisis* that depended heavily on the imagination's capacities for self-othering and self-gathering. The purpose of *oikeoisis* seems to have been to engage the mind in both the local and natural commonwealths at once. The trick was to imagine oneself poised at the center of a network of concentric circles, wherein each circle represented a relationship one had to the wider world. Then one would try to gather as many of the outer circles toward the center as possible, going about it systematically, first coming to terms with oneself as the nucleus of the world-network, then moving out one circle to the family, then out one more to the city, then to the empire, continent, and so on, past the stars and heavens, until the person at the center, like the sun, had touched the outermost concentricities of the cosmos with his thoughts. A properly conducted *oikeoisis* (the word comes from the Greek *oikos*, meaning household or family), familiarized everything existing, the endgame being to gain as profound a partiality toward the things remote from oneself as the things nearby.

O

If the ancients performed their cosmopolitanism through an *oikeoisis* or compression of cosmological space, their modern Western counterparts did something comparable with regard to historical time. Born of an age of unprecedented geopolitical intimacy, modern cosmopolitans were less obsessed with bridging wide tracts of cosmological space than with bridging temporal gaps in human evolution. Their conviction that different peoples dwelled contemporaneously at different stages of human development led them to contrive the concept of *universal history* as a modern correlative to the ancient commonwealth of the sun. The idea of a universal natural history with a cosmopolitan purpose, as Immanuel Kant once called it, was an ambitious new proposal for integrating "modern" and "premodern" human formations into a single temporal continuum tending toward a conclusion that had the same significance for all.

The idea that a natural temporal continuum bound a universal humanity together first of all assumed that the same concept of humanity would signify felicitously the world over. Out of this first assumption, a second followed, namely, that humanity had an historical purpose on the level of the species– maturation toward a fully enlightened intelligence– even if the signs of that enlightenment were not yet manifest in every locale. Third, universal history negated diachronic, non-eurocentric temporalities from historical accounting, interpreting the history of the human species from the vantage point of European modernity (Immanuel Kant once said that history began in the far-flung parts of the world only after Europe had arrived on their shores). What all of this amounted to was a forced integration of historically disparate modes of being, along with their corresponding cosmologies, into a linear temporal system that understood human experience as a progression in stages from barbarism to rational enlightenment. The story of humanity, as Friedrich Schiller would put it summarily, was the story of an "unsociable troglodyte" becoming a "cultured man of the world." (*Troglodytae*, "cave dwellers," was a name the ancient Greeks once gave to an ancient Ethiopian tribe.)

0

Climatological determinism explained how different human groups found themselves in different stages of progress when modernity dawned in Europe. Local meteorology, essentially, was thought to have a powerful determining effect on the progress of rationality within different cultural formations. Europe's rational vanguardism was understood in large part as an effect of its temperate climes. Four distinct seasons, including bitter winters and mild summers, steeled the European's thinking and varied his passions, forming him well for a self-starting life of intellect and industry. Peoples of tropical, desert, or extreme intemperate climates were comparatively less fortunate when it came to the natural distribution of cognitive resources. Overmuch exposure to sunlight or inclement weather dulled their minds' deliberative faculties, making southern peoples more prone than northerners to irrationality and indolence. The modern cosmopolitans were optimistic, however, that the increasing geopolitical contact between Europe and the rest of the world would heal the uneven natural development that divided modernity from its others. The idea of a universal history with a cosmopolitan conclusion presented an opportunity for peoples everywhere, including the hyper-rational moderns of the temperate zones, to overcome their local determinations once and for all and realize freedom in the widest possible sense:

> Mankind has intermingled the regions and the seasons, and has toughened the weak plants of the Orient to his own harsh climate. As he brought Europe to the West Indies and the South Seas, so he also let Asia arise in Europe. A merrier sky now laughs above Germany's forests, which the powerful hand of man tore open to the rays of sunshine, and in the waves of the Rhine are mirrored Asia's grapevines.

Perhaps it was naive of Friedrich Schiller, the author of these prescient lines, to think that Europe could assimilate the natural wonders of Asia, Africa, and the Americas, more often than not by force, without also considering whether the "merrier" global skies now laughing over Europe's forests might one day have the last laugh over them. His penchant for naturalistic metaphors to describe the unification of diverse cultural groupings suggests that his cosmopolitanism was more aesthetically than politically calculated. Indeed, he seems to have allowed his imagination to regard the unaccounted-for range of human formations around the world as a bourgeois might regard his own private garden.

0

A botanical education center belonging to the Friedrich Schiller Universität in Jena, Germany, illustrates the elective affinity between modern cosmopolitanism and curatorial gardening. The research complex is an amalgam of climate-controlled greenhouses and open-air gardens, with guided tours and walking routes that make the indoor and outdoor spaces seem part of a continuous aesthetic experience. Desert, tropic, tundra, German or Japanese pastoral: all find representation somewhere in the gardens.

As best it can, the botanical center tries to make the goals of science and art complementary. The indoor houses are designed to conceal the tools of research and maintenance as much as possible. In the tropics room, for example, a ladder leading up to the elevated watering platform has vines twisting through it that let it function as a host tree would. In the neighboring hydroponics room, blue and green dyes stain the surfaces of the growing ponds, discretely submerging water pumps, thermometers, and pH meters in a wash of color. The aim of these aesthetic concealments is not to erase the signs of human intervention (a botanical garden never pretends to be an uncultivated natural space). The aim, rather, is to let the concept of a globally sourced garden make an immediate impression on the viewer, putting the emphasis on the overall harmony of the design, rather than the tedious technical maintenance it requires to keep the harmony intact. The impression left is that of an Eden revived by man's own hand–modernity returning to prehistory, so to speak, with a mixed feeling of wonder and understanding.

The outdoor gardens are in some ways better suited to the botanical center's mission than the indoor ones. Already fitted to Germany's temperate local climate, the integrated collections of native and exotic plants mingle with less artifice here than in any other area of the complex. It is outdoors, as well, that the taxonomical mission of the gardens is most on display. The little white stakes stuck next to each unique plant species let visitors know the name of the plant they are looking at, where on the globe it comes from, and what its German nickname is. Nowhere is this taxonomic system more conspicuous than in a rock garden of miniscule alpine plants, all individually labeled, that grow like uncut hairs out of fissures in the rocks. It is an eloquent testament to the garden's exhaustive curatorial efforts: care for the *infinitesimal* is at the heart of the botanical cosmopolitanism on display. In the case of the alpine rock plants, it would not be an exaggeration to say that the signs are as important as the things signified. Calling out every plant species, however small, by its proper name puts the gardener's worldliness as much on display as nature's variety.

0

Unheimlich is the name of a recent summer exhibition at Universität Leipzig that collects the field notes and textbooks of German anthropologists who were some of the first Europeans to explore the world's equatorial rainforests for the purpose of gathering information about nonhuman primates. If *Unheimlich* stresses one theme above others, it is the unseemly takeover of disinterested scientific inquiry about humanity and its nearest relatives by anthropocentric and eurocentric tropes. The exhibition is both a retrospective of the great scientific strides made during the Enlightenment period and a reckoning with the unscientific racism of pre-, and to a large extent, post-Darwinian theories of evolution.

A generic late seventeenth-century textbook provides a good example of the problems then plaguing the new science of man. The book opens to a page displaying profiles of three humanoid heads arranged in a vertical series suggesting evolutionary ascent: the bottom profile shows a bearded pre-human primate with a prominent brow and a jaw that juts out perpendicularly from the face; the middle one, a human being of African descent, bald-headed and beardless, with a slightly more receded jaw; the top profile, a human being of European descent, drawn in the style of classical Greco-Roman sculpture, the forehead coiffed with curls, the chin now receding into symmetric alignment with the brow. A note off to the side of the display explains how some scientists of the period speculated that the property of reason first emerged in "man" when his mouth receded behind his nose, thereby aligning the speech organs with the brain.

On display as well, in a far corner of the room, are a few artistic renderings of the German anthropologists' findings–assorted drawings, paintings, and miniatures that communicate the aesthetic import of the new science. One series of illustrations shows various species of nonhuman primates sitting in what could be taken as traditional portrait poses. The portraits, if that is what they are, exploit the full range of bourgeois parlor-room semiotics. A chimpanzee with enormous ears and slightly shrugging shoulders turns bashfully away from the viewer, as if caught gazing in adoration. An orangutan with an upturned smile appears lost in a solitary reverie, suggesting a lurid secret withheld. Transplanted into the foyer of an aristocratic estate, or hung above a mantle in a sitting room, the impression left by these portraits would indeed be *unheimlich*–comically so. These downright impish primate faces, onto which the artist has projected all the subtleties of the human visage, remind modern science of what humanity will have to give back to nature after desacralizing its concept.

0

For some time now the lakes at Regent's Park, London, have been used as the main breeding areas for the Royal Parks' globally curated ornamental waterfowl collection. The breeding program serves the eight major parks within the Greater London network, bringing together a hundred species of swans, geese, and ducks, native to every continent in the world, into a monitored habitat designed to accommodate as many of their natural reproductive needs as possible. The scene is almost reminiscent of

Aristophanes' classical comedy *The Birds*, in which a diverse alliance of bird species—with the help of a few human infiltrators disguised in wings—founds a pan-avian republic that exiles gods and humans alike from its ranks. The chorus leader of the new republic tells his human counterparts that if they should recognize the birds as the new gods in town, the birds will in turn render humans the service of marking the seasons, announcing spring, summer, autumn, and winter individually, so that humans will know when to sow or reap their wheat, breed or sequester their livestock, weave warm or light clothing, and so on.

Supposing for a moment that such an arrangement did obtain between birds and humans, what exactly would the white-and-black smew, a native of northern Eurasia and Siberia, signal to the casual visitor of Regent's Park in June? The smew's normal habit in the wild would be to pass the summer months at a cool lake in Scandinavia, dining on the fish and larvae hatches there, before migrating in winter to the frigid Baltic to hunker down for breeding. Here, though, in the semi-captivity of the Royal Parks, he seems content to forfeit his migratory habits for a life of drifting idly on the boating lakes. Eating and breeding are no longer cyclical struggles for him. He has taken rather well to bourgeois city life. (Is there no winter in his native range that compares with an English summer?)

From the top of Parliament Hill on Hampstead Heath, where, on an overcast afternoon, London looks smothered in ash and light, it is hard to imagine a modest river like the River Thames overwhelming a city of this scale with stormwater. And yet it has happened several times. History reports that London can flood as miserably as it burns. In the past the Thames has tended to be a winter flooder, its banks swelling around Christmas or New Year's with the sudden melt of a Cotswold blizzard, dumping its fatal sludge on the streets and tenements of central London with a fury resembling that of a much mightier river.

No doubt the Thames draws much of its threatening power from the skies above London. The daily transactions between river and sky generate a spectrum of chilled, northern-isle colors that permeate the city, even in summer: blues tinged with something leaden or metallic, grays layered inside of profounder grays. Each hue brings a distinctive temperature and mood to its corner of the urban canvass; each seems mutable by infinite subtle degrees. *Now coldness; now melancholia; now that weird English cheerfulness*. The unshakeable feeling of dread emanating from these color-moods owes in part to their vaporous shapeshifting. Stared at long enough, they become loosened from their earthly context, turning London into a kinetic color study seemingly without a material host.

Tayeb Salih's *Season of Migration to the North*, a novel set in a postcolonial Sudan of the 1960s, is in large part a meditation on the legacy of a Western cosmopolitan education in an Islamic agrarian civilization organized temporally around the Nile River's summer flood patterns. The narrative is framed by the voice of a nameless first-person narrator, an Arabic-speaking Sudanese man trained in advanced literary studies at a top university in England, who finds himself in existential peril when his friend and adversary, the only other English-educated Sudanese he knows in his home village, dies, "by drowning or suicide," in the Nile River. Of his friend's mysterious death he observes that

> Nature had bestowed upon him the very end which he would have wanted for himself. Imagine: the height of summer in the month of fateful July; the indifferent river has flooded as never before in thirty years; the darkness has fused all the elements of nature into one single neutral one, older than the river itself and more indifferent. But was it really the end he was looking for? Perhaps he wanted it to happen in the north, the far north, on a stormy, icy night, under a starless sky, among a people to whom he did not matter—

These reflections are in near-perfect symmetry with the final scene of the novel, where the narrator, distressed by the sinister lingering of his friend's memory months after his death, decides to go for a mind-cleansing swim in the Nile. His sensations upon entering the water are those of a man grieving; he is in between everything and unsure of anything. It is a symbolic summary of his life in Sudan after returning from seven years (the time it took him to complete his doctorate and not a day longer) in England. He missed his home terribly during that time, he tells his reader. By returning he had hoped that the ice that had formed in his heart while abroad would melt in the liquid warmth of his native tribe. And yet he had returned to Sudan a man of the so-called "wider world." Now he finds that the execution of his bureaucratic duties for the new Ministry of Education does little to mitigate the harshness of his village's agrarian existence. Nor do the reams of English Romantic poetry he has committed to memory give him access to the inner movements of his own heart. He does not know whether he admires or hates his dead friend; whether he sympathizes with or resents his English educators. As he swims further out into the current, he notes how the Nile's gently reverberating waters make him feel at once worldly and worldless, awake and asleep. By the time he reaches the midpoint between the north and south banks of the river, he has become physically exhausted with ambivalence. "In a state between life and death," he writes, his body bobbing limply in the current,

I saw formations of sand grouse heading northwards.
Were we in winter or summer? Was it a casual flight
or a migration?

Winter or summer–a peculiar question to put to
oneself during a life-and-death struggle. (Would the
question be as urgent for him had he not lived for a
winter in London?) At any rate he does not try to
answer it. Instead, he describes his struggle to swim
on, to break out of his cycle of indecision for good:

> Like a comic actor shouting on a stage, I screamed
> with all my remaining strength, 'Help! Help!'

0

So fails the summer. Christina Rossetti's
"Remember Me," the poetic complement of
her "Dream-Love," is a rendition of summer's
concession speech to winter as it bows to autumn.
The poem reads like an outpouring of melancholy
after a long comic evasion:

> Remember me when I am gone away,
>> Gone far away into the silent land;
>> When you can no more hold me by the hand,
> Nor I half turn to go yet turning stay.
> Remember me when no more day by day
>> You tell me of our future that you plann'd:
>> Only remember me; you understand
> It will be late to counsel then or pray.
> Yet if you should forget me for a while
>> And afterwards remember, do not grieve:

For if the darkness and corruption leave
A vestige of the thoughts that once I had,
Better by far you should forget and smile
Than that you should remember and be sad.

It would be a full concession speech if summer would encourage autumn to grieve for it as a truly departed object. Once again, though, Christina Rossetti's seeming melancholy turns out a piercing comic insight. The puckish poet's final trick for the young dreamer is to utter "remember" in the imperative tense while discouraging memorialization altogether.

1

Summer, a dream, then autumn, again. It is a clear October evening in Columbus, Ohio, fifty-five degrees, a faint breeze blowing. A gardener is hurriedly raking twigs and fallen leaves out of the flowerbeds under the monument in Schiller Park, trying to get his work done before dark. The flowerbeds, diamond-shaped, bordered with low hedges, are dormant except for a cluster of pale yellow bearded irises blooming out of the center of one of the diamonds. They are a type of reblooming iris that appears once in the first weeks of spring, withers before summer, then reappears for a second bloom in late autumn, well after the first night chills have taken out the other seasonal flowers. Their corollas have the papyrus-like texture of an ordinary iris with some added delicate ruffling around the edges. Their nickname: summer olympics. A number of reblooming irises have nicknames like this: *summer olympics, autumn jester, immortality,* titles that allude to the flowers' clever evasion of the estival months.

After clearing the last beds of dead leaves, the gardener circles back to check on the progress of his irises. He removes his work gloves and uses the forefinger and thumb of his left hand to gently pinch the "beards," the elongated styles, of the corollas, as if to probe their remaining strength. The tongue-shaped petals are starting to shrivel somewhat now that November is almost arrived. Likely the next deep chill will start the process of turning them brown. The rot will start along the outer edges of the petals, spreading inward to their supple centers. Then the blooms will lose their upright bearing altogether and begin flaking off layers like snakes shedding their skins. But that eventuality is still a few nights off. For now, the gardener's gentle handling restores some needed tension to the irises' slackening beards, lending them a pinch of strength to stand up to the cold dews coming overnight.

Michael Skelton
Nashville, Tennessee

WORKS CITED BY MICHAEL SKELTON

Spring, Anew (2014)

John Keats, 'To Autumn,' http://www.poets.org/ poetsorg/poem/autumn; Henry David Thoreau, *Walden and Civil Disobedience*, Barnes & Noble Classics, New York, 2003; René Descartes, *Meditations on First Philosophy*, Hackett Publishing Company, Indianapolis, 1993; Ralph Ellison, *Invisible Man*, Vintage International, New York, 1980; Wallace Stevens, *The Collected Poems*, Vintage Books, New York, 1982.

Estival (2017)

Claude Monet, "Morning on the Seine in Giverny" and "Ice Floes," Metropolitan Museum of Art, New York City; William Shakespeare, *A Midsummer Night's Dream*, http://shakespeare.mit.edu/midsummer/full.html; Christina Rossetti, *Poems*, Everyman's Library, 1993; Seneca, *Moral and Political Writings*, Cambridge University Press, 2010; Cicero, *On Duties*, Cambridge University Press, 1990; Immanuel Kant, *Kant's Political Writings*, Cambridge University Press, 1990; Friedrich Schiller, "What is, and to what end, do we study universal history?", https://www.schillerinstitute.org/transl/Schiller_essays/ universal_history.html; Aristophanes, *The Birds*, http:// classics.mit.edu/Aristophanes/birds.html; Tayeb Salih, *Season of Migration to the North*, NYRB Classics, 2009.

www.ingramcontent.com/pod-product-compliance
Lightning Source LLC
Chambersburg PA
CBHW051734040426
42447CB00008B/1126